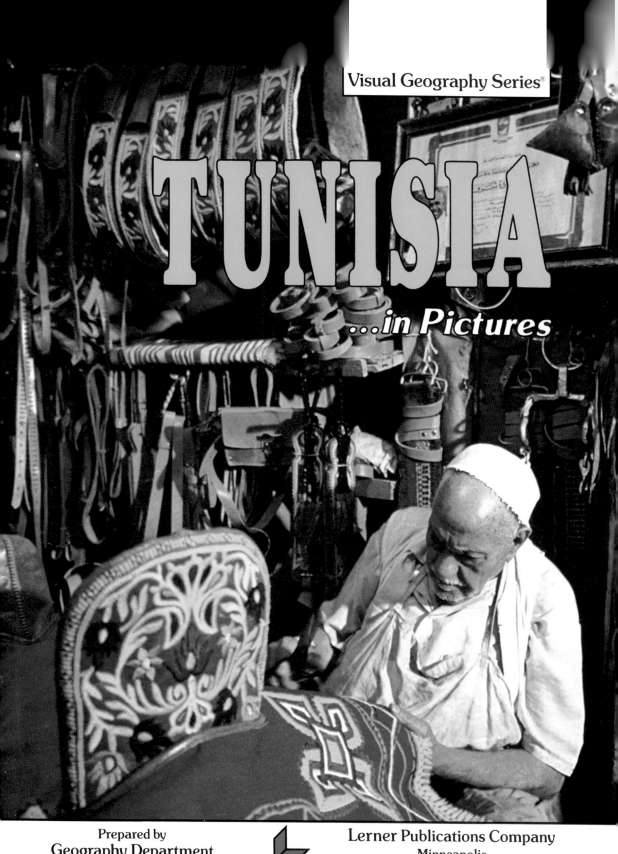

Visual Geography Series®

TUNISIA
...in Pictures

Prepared by
Geography Department

Lerner Publications Company
Minneapolis

Independent Picture Service

These Tunisian girls carry collapsible baskets that will be used to crush oil from olives.

This is an all-new edition of the Visual Geography Series. Previous editions have been published by Sterling Publishing Company, New York City, and some of the original textual information has been retained. New photographs, maps, charts, captions, and updated information have been added. The text has been entirely reset in 10/12 Century Textbook.

LIBRARY OF CONGRESS CATALOGING-IN-PUBLICATION DATA

Tunisia in pictures / prepared by Geography
  Department, Lerner Publications Company.
    p.   cm.—(Visual geography series)
  Rev. ed. of: Tunisia in pictures / by Coleman Lollar.
  Includes index.
  Summary: Introduces the land, history, government, people, and economy of the North African country that was once the site of the ancient city of Carthage.
  ISBN 0-8225-1844-9
  1. Tunisia. [1. Tunisia.] I. Lollar, Coleman. Tunisia in pictures. II. Lerner Publications Company. Geography Dept. III. Series: Visual geography series (Minneapolis, Minn.)
DT245.T7957 1989
961'.105—dc19   88–12965
                                                 CIP
                                                 AC

International Standard Book Number: 0-8225-1844-9
Library of Congress Catalog Card Number: 88-12965

VISUAL GEOGRAPHY SERIES®

Publisher
Harry Jonas Lerner
Associate Publisher
Nancy M. Campbell
Senior Editor
Mary M. Rodgers
Editor
Gretchen Bratvold
Assistant Editors
Dan Filbin
Kathleen S. Heidel
Photo Researcher
Karen A. Sirvaitis
Editorial/Photo Assistant
Marybeth Campbell
Consultants/Contributors
Isaac Eshel
Sandra K. Davis
Designer
Jim Simondet
Cartographer
Carol F. Barrett
Indexer
Sylvia Timian
Production Manager
Richard J. Hannah

Independent Picture Service

For centuries the fertile soil around the Gulf of Tunis has attracted people to this coastal region.

Acknowledgments

Title page photo courtesy of Tunisian National Tourist Office, Tunis.

Elevation contours adapted from *The Times Atlas of the World*, seventh comprehensive edition (New York: Times Books, 1985).

1 2 3 4 5 6 7 8 9 10 98 97 96 95 94 93 92 91 90 89

Courtyards – open areas surrounded by walls or sleeping quarters – are common features of Tunisian homes. The space serves as a kitchen, dining room, and living room. Some dwellings have stairs that lead to a flat roof where the family can store food and spread out grains in the sun to dry.

Contents

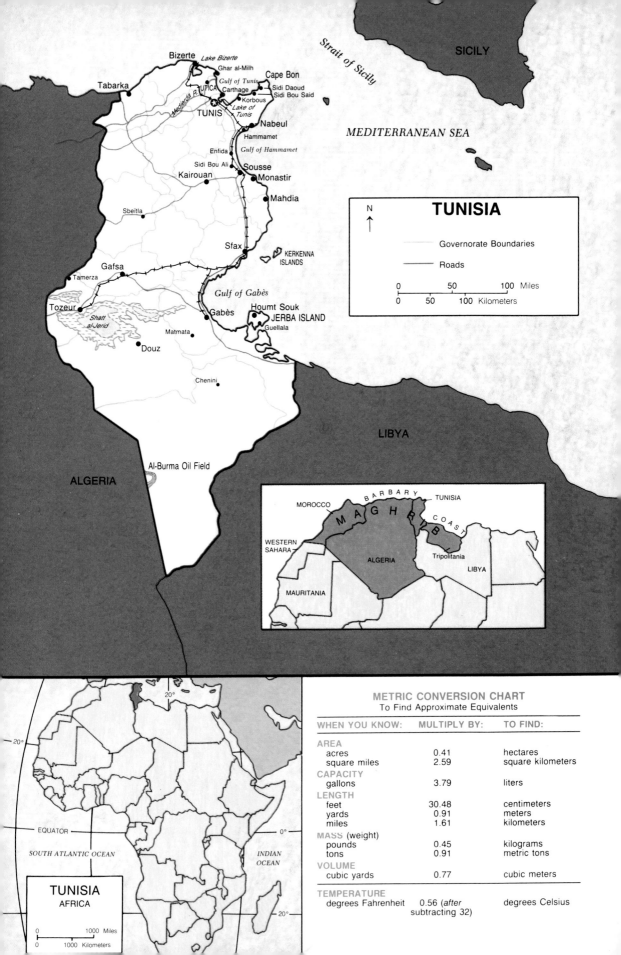

TUNISIA

N ↑

— Governorate Boundaries
— Roads

| 0 | 50 | 100 Miles |
| 0 | 50 | 100 Kilometers |

MEDITERRANEAN SEA

Strait of Sicily

SICILY

Bizerte · Lake Bizerte
Ghar al-Milh
Cape Bon
Tabarka
Gulf of Tunis
UTICA · Carthage · Sidi Daoud · Sidi Bou Said
Medjerda R. · Korbous
TUNIS · Lake of Tunis
Nabeul
Hammamet
Enfida · Gulf of Hammamet
Sidi Bou Ali · Sousse
Kairouan · Monastir
Mahdia
Sbeitla
Sfax
KERKENNA ISLANDS
Gafsa
Tamerza
Gulf of Gabès
Tozeur
Shatt al-Jerid
Gabès · Houmt Souk · JERBA ISLAND · Guellala
Matmata
Douz
Chenini

LIBYA

ALGERIA

Al-Burma Oil Field

MAGHRIB
BARBARY COAST
MOROCCO
TUNISIA
WESTERN SAHARA
ALGERIA
Tripolitania
LIBYA
MAURITANIA

20°
20°
EQUATOR
0°
SOUTH ATLANTIC OCEAN
INDIAN OCEAN
20°

TUNISIA
AFRICA

| 0 | 1000 Miles |
| 0 | 1000 Kilometers |

METRIC CONVERSION CHART
To Find Approximate Equivalents

WHEN YOU KNOW:	MULTIPLY BY:	TO FIND:
AREA		
acres	0.41	hectares
square miles	2.59	square kilometers
CAPACITY		
gallons	3.79	liters
LENGTH		
feet	30.48	centimeters
yards	0.91	meters
miles	1.61	kilometers
MASS (weight)		
pounds	0.45	kilograms
tons	0.91	metric tons
VOLUME		
cubic yards	0.77	cubic meters
TEMPERATURE		
degrees Fahrenheit	0.56 (*after* subtracting 32)	degrees Celsius

Good harbors along the Tunisian coast have attracted foreigners to the region since the twelfth century B.C., when Phoenician merchants established trade with local peoples. The Romans came to the area several centuries later, and magnificent architectural remains, such as this amphitheater, attest to the Roman presence in Tunisia.

Introduction

Surrounded by ocean and desert, Tunisia lies within the Maghrib—the name given to northwestern Africa by Islamic conquerors in the seventh century A.D. Arab influence in the region is strong, but because Tunisia is situated just 90 miles from the European island of Sicily, the nation is a popular trading partner and tourist area for Europeans.

Tunisia's location on the African continent at a point where European, African, and Arabic cultures meet has shaped its history. For thousands of years, invaders came from the north (Romans), from the

5

east (Arabs and Ottoman Turks), from the south (Berbers), and from the west (the French). The nation's population represents a mixture of these peoples with the local inhabitants. Among the country's numerous archaeological sites is the ancient Phoenician city of Carthage, which stands as evidence of the region's past glory.

The Arab-Islamic conquest of the territory during the seventh century left a lasting imprint on Tunisia. Yet Western influence, which was introduced during the French colonial period from 1881 to 1956, has set the nation apart from other Arab states that have remained more traditional. Much of Tunisia's modernization was paved by one man—Habib Bourguiba—who guided the country's struggle for independence and who led the new government during its first 31 years.

President Bourguiba favored gradual, Western-style development. As his regime became more entrenched, however, he allowed fewer and fewer people to criticize him. In the 1970s and 1980s unrest broke out as inflation and unemployment rates increased. Amid a rising tide of popular discontent, Bourguiba was ousted from power on November 7, 1987, by Prime

At an outdoor market, weavers bargain for wool, which they will turn into blankets and into cloth for traditional Tunisian garments. The craft industry plays an important role in the nation's economy.

Minister Zine al-Abidine ben Ali, who assumed control of the government. Although ben Ali faces severe economic problems and potential opposition from religious conservatives, many Tunisians view the takeover with optimism.

Along tree-lined Avenue Habib Bourguiba in Tunis, the nation's capital, Eastern and Western cultures meet. Tunisians clothed in traditional Arab styles walk beside people who have adopted Western dress. Foreign embassies, sidewalk cafés, and boutiques stand next to Arab teahouses, Tunisian art galleries, and the gate to the medina—the old Arab quarter.

The Gulf of Hammamet, sometimes referred to as the Tunisian riviera (coastal resort region), curves along fertile land where tall cypress trees shade fruit orchards. The town of Hammamet, a walled village flanked by fine sand beaches, is one of Tunisia's largest resorts.

1) The Land

Bounded on the west by Algeria, on the south and southeast by Libya, and on the north and northeast by the Mediterranean Sea, Tunisia lies at the midpoint of the North African coast. Cape Bon, a peninsula in northeastern Tunisia, divides the Mediterranean into eastern and western halves. The narrow Strait of Sicily connects the two portions of the sea between Cape Bon and the Italian island of Sicily 90 miles to the northeast.

With 63,378 square miles of territory, the Republic of Tunisia is slightly smaller than the state of Missouri. The country has 1,000 miles of Mediterranean coastline, which accounts for nearly half of its borders. Three large gulfs indent the Tunisian coastline, providing excellent natural anchorages for commercial boats and warships since ancient times. On the north is the Gulf of Tunis, which takes its name from the republic's capital city. Facing eastward are the Gulfs of Hammamet and Gabès. Tunisia's territory also includes several islands that lie near the mainland. The most important are the Kerkenna Islands and subtropical Jerba Island, both of which lie in the Gulf of Gabès.

Topography

Tunisia rises gradually in altitude from east to west and becomes more arid in the south. Three geographic regions—northern highlands, central steppes (plains), and southern desert—characterize Tunisia's landscape.

HIGHLANDS

The northern quarter of Tunisia is known as the Tell, or highlands. The Dorsale, meaning "backbone," separates the Tell from the rest of the country and contains a few peaks that reach an elevation of about 5,000 feet—the highest altitude in the country.

In both the Dorsale and the Tell, the highest areas are near the Algerian border,

7

where they merge with the Atlas Mountains. This chain rises to the west and dominates the North African landscape all the way to the Atlantic coast in Morocco. Unlike the sharp, rugged Atlas chain, however, Tunisia's highlands consist of soft sandstones and clays and have a rounded outline. In the northern Tell, adequate amounts of rainfall support forests and vineyards. Farther south the highlands are chalk-white and lifeless.

In the west the Tell contains rolling hills and rich green valleys. Near the northeastern Gulf of Tunis, from the city of Bizerte to Cape Bon, the land is lower and flatter than the rest of the Tell. Because of its wet climate and fertile soil, the Tell supports varied agricultural development as well as the majority of Tunisia's population. Indeed, more than 50 percent of the population lives in the Tell, which covers only 20 percent of Tunisia's total area.

STEPPES

South of the Dorsale are the steppes, a semi-arid region where rock and sand alternate with grasses and olive trees. With irrigation these plains can produce crops, and they have sustained a sizable population since the Romans arrived in the second century B.C.

Subdivided into three sections, the region encompasses the High Steppes in the west, the Low Steppes in the central portion, and the Sahel along the eastern coast. This latter plain is known for its fine olive groves. Running about 200 miles from north to south, the Sahel has two distinct areas—one that is well watered along the Gulf of Hammamet and the lower, drier re-

The northern town of Korbous is nestled among hills that descend into the Gulf of Tunis. Tunisia's northern region is more fertile and more mountainous than the rest of the country.

Courtesy of Tunisian National Tourist Office, Tunis

Although the steppes are generally quite dry, seasonal streams water some places, such as Tamerza in the western High Steppes.

South of the steppes is the beginning of Tunisia's desert region—an extension of the Sahara Desert. The Sahara covers about one-fourth of Africa, and only a tiny portion of its expanse lies within the boundaries of Tunisia. Drifting sand dunes and rocky, uneven surfaces interrupted by mountainous ridges, such as the Ksour Mountains, compose much of Tunisia's desert terrain. A sandy portion that extends from central Algeria into southwestern Tunisia is called the Great Eastern Erg.

Sources of Water

Tunisia's only important river with a year-round supply of water is the Medjerda, which begins in the highlands of northern Algeria. The waterway flows northeast, depositing rich sediments along its path before emptying into the Mediterranean near Ghar al-Milh. Other rivers are seasonal and are completely dry much of the year. Throughout the Arab world, such streams and their dry beds are called wadis.

Just south of the steppes, separating Tunisia's northern regions from the Sahara, lies Shatt al-Jerid, a large, shallow salt lake covering 1,900 square miles. Shatt al-Jerid at times loses most of its

gion south of the gulf, around the city of Sfax. The Sahel includes the Jerba and Kerkenna islands in the Gulf of Gabès.

Sand dunes typify the Great Eastern Erg, which extends into southwestern Tunisia.

Courtesy of Tunisian National Tourist Office, Tunis

9

Independent Picture Service

Camels drink refreshing water at the town of Douz near Shatt al-Jerid. One of a few oases (fertile areas) in the Tunisian desert, Douz grows date palms.

water through evaporation and nearly becomes a salt plain.

Geologists believe that Shatt al-Jerid and many smaller shatts (salt marshes) nearby were once part of the Gulf of Gabès. A narrow strip of land that joins the steppes with the desert cuts off the shatts from the Mediterranean. Because Shatt al-Jerid lies at one of the lowest points in Tunisia, it has an extensive drainage system that captures moisture from hundreds of miles of surrounding territory. High ground around the shatts supports oases (fertile areas), where date palms thrive. This far south, however, rain seldom amounts to very much, and for long periods the shatts may lack any source of water.

Climate

Two important factors influence Tunisia's climate. The Mediterranean provides moisture and relatively cool breezes in the north, and the Sahara sends dry, hot winds across the south. The northern coast has a pleasant climate and receives more rainfall than other areas in Tunisia. Farther south the air becomes hotter and drier.

Tunisia has three major climatic regions that mirror the topography. The country's northern quarter enjoys typical Mediterranean weather, with cool, rainy winters and hot, dry summers. Temperatures in this region average about 45° F in January and 80° F in July. The coast, however, is slightly warmer in winter and cooler in summer. The central area is classified as savanna (grassland)—an arid, mid-latitude region with hot summers, mild winters, and very little precipitation. The desert climate of the south receives almost no rainfall and experiences hotter summers and colder winters than the rest of the country. Summer temperatures often exceed 100° F, and occasionally water freezes in the winter.

Rainfall varies in Tunisia from 20 to 25 inches annually in the north to zero in the south. Tunis, the capital, receives about 22

A community development worker visits a woman living in Enfida, inland from the Gulf of Hammamet. The Tunisian government has improved living conditions in many rural areas by replacing mud-brick houses with prefabricated, permanent structures and by digging deeper wells so that water supplies will outlast long dry periods.

inches of rain each year. The high Dorsale acts as the land's most influential climate barrier, blocking the south from the north's rain and cool air. Along the northern and eastern coasts, local sea breezes bring rain and cool air, but along the Gulf of Gabès and in the south, the breezes yield to desert heat just a few miles inland. In the far west, high altitudes help to lower the temperatures.

Natural Resources

Unlike neighboring Libya and Algeria, Tunisia has not become a major producer of the world's oil. Indeed, Tunisia did not export its first shipment of oil until 1966. Large quantities of petroleum may lie under the desert sands, but Tunisians have only begun to explore the reserves, such as those at the Al-Burma oil field. The shifting dunes of the Great Eastern Erg make drilling difficult throughout much of the south. Since 1949 Tunisia has produced enough natural gas from its

wells on Cape Bon to meet the energy needs of the population of Tunis.

The hills of the Dorsale provide abundant supplies of low-grade phosphate and a somewhat limited amount of high-grade iron ore. Tunisia has constructed several chemical plants to process phosphate into fertilizer, making the mineral more valuable and easier to export. An oversupply on the world market, however, has decreased the value of phosphate. In addition to phosphate and iron ore, there are small supplies of lead, zinc, potash, and mercury.

Flora and Fauna

Tunisia has three major flora and fauna regions that parallel the climatic regions. The north supports natural Mediterranean vegetation as well as agricultural crops such as wheat, olives, and fruit trees, especially citrus. Evergreen forests of cork oaks, pines, and pistachio trees thrive in Tunisia's well-watered Tell. On many

11

of these hills, grapes grow abundantly. Throughout the central region, seasonal vegetation, such as alfa grass—which is used as pulp in paper manufacturing—and olive and acacia trees are common. The south supports almost no plant life at all. Along the coasts and at desert oases, such as Gafsa and Gabès, date palms and other fruit trees grow.

Tunisia's wildlife is concentrated in the north. Jackals and wild boars roam the forested areas of the Tell, and gazelles and wild sheep wander the Dorsale. Scorpions, horned vipers, and other dangerous reptiles are among the few wild creatures that inhabit the southern desert. Camels are the most important domestic animals throughout Tunisia, because of their ability to transport loads for many days without drinking water. Sheep, goats, and sheepdogs are also found throughout Tunisia.

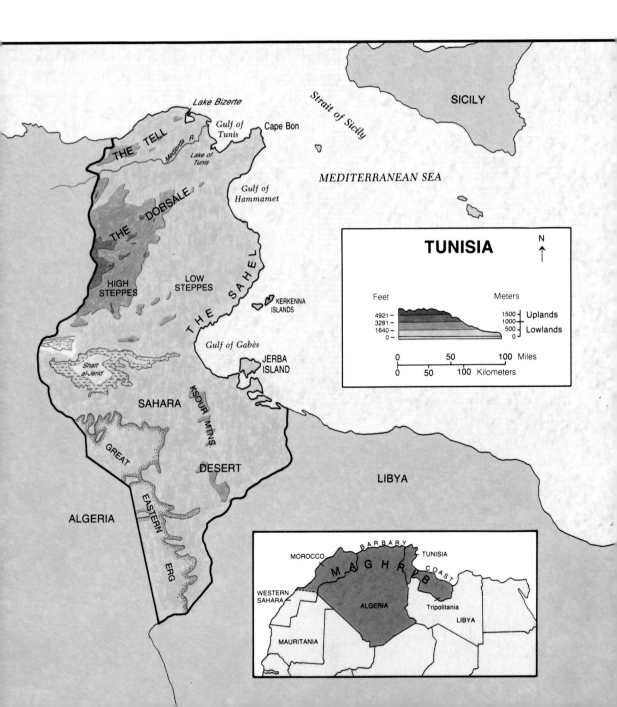

Cacti—found in many of Tunisia's dry areas—adapt to arid conditions by storing water in their fleshy stems. Most cacti have a very short blooming cycle. The flowers last only a few days, which prevents water from evaporating from the large, soft petals.

Courtesy of Tunisian National Tourist Office, Tunis

The country's birdlife includes flamingos and storks along the coasts and in the north. Buzzards—large birds of prey—inhabit the south. The waters off Tunisia's coast support abundant sea life. Fishermen catch lobster, giltheads, red mullets, octopuses, sponges, and tuna for local and foreign markets.

Large, sociable water birds, flamingos average about five feet in height. Because they are best suited to secluded habitats, urban expansion threatens their existence.

Photo by Marty Schneider

The minaret (a tower from which followers of the Islamic religion are called to prayer) of a mosque rises prominently in the medina of Tunis.

Tunis

Tunis, the city from which the country takes its name, is the governmental, economic, and commercial capital of the nation. A metropolis of about one million people, Tunis lies near the site of the ancient Phoenician city of Carthage. Tunis probably arose in the sixth century B.C. as a Phoenician settlement, though its historical importance began only in the seventh century A.D.

Located on an isthmus—a narrow strip of land—Tunis lies between two lagoons, with the Lake of Tunis to the east. The narrow, winding streets of the old, walled section are lined with many suqs (outdoor markets) and mosques (Islamic houses of worship). The French built the modern section of Tunis during their period of rule from 1881 to 1956.

Although square, one-story buildings still cover Tunis as they have for centuries, a new, tall skyline is taking shape in the

Each street of Tunis's medina specializes in the sale of a particular line of products. Tunisians can buy clothes at this suq (market).

14

city. Today Tunis is the country's most important port and the home of its finest cultural institutions, including the Bardo Museum. Roman ruins and sunny beaches nearby have helped to make Tunis one of Africa's most popular tourist cities.

Secondary Cities

Sfax (population 375,000), the second largest urban area in Tunisia, is an industrial town and port on the Gulf of Gabès. The city wall dates from the ninth century A.D., and most residents that are not employed by chemical plants are either fishermen or olive growers.

Eighty miles north of Sfax lies Sousse (population 300,000), the third largest urban area in Tunisia. A Phoenician town on the Gulf of Hammamet, Sousse has served merchants since the days of Carthage. Still a thriving port, the city has evolved into a resort area. Several luxury hotels rise along the white beaches. Much of the city was bombed during World War II, but the modern section has been rebuilt, and the old quarter has been carefully restored.

Bizerte, 40 miles north of Tunis and the northernmost town in Africa, is an industrial center and seaport with a population of about 95,000. The town's location on the Mediterranean and its three natural harbors—including the deep, landlocked lagoon of Lake Bizerte—have attracted settlers since early Roman days. The French maintained an arsenal and a naval base at this strategic point until 1963.

Kairouan (population 72,000), an interior city about 75 miles south of Tunis, is a religious center of North Africa. The first Islamic capital of the Maghrib, Kairouan was founded in A.D. 670 and became a center of Arab civilization in 800. The city is famous for its fine mosques, as well as for the wool carpets that weavers in the area have produced for hundreds of years.

Gabès (population 93,000) is a lush oasis by the sea, where fruit trees and date palms grow in startling contrast to the barren land that surrounds the city. Air pollution from nearby chemical complexes and water pollution in local streams have spoiled the natural beauty of Gabès.

Gafsa (population 60,000) is Tunisia's northernmost oasis city, located 75 miles inland from Gabès. Long known for the tropical crops that rely on its springs, the city has become a hub of phosphate mining and serves as an administrative center for southwestern Tunisia.

Beyond the Great Mosque in Sousse stretches the harbor, from which salt and agricultural products of the Sahel are exported.

Courtesy of Tunisian National Tourist Office, Tunis

15

Photo by Drs. A. A. M. van der Heyden, Naarden, the Netherlands

Although the Phoenician queen Dido founded Carthage in the ninth century B.C., most of the remains in the area—including this statue—date from the Roman period, which began in 146 B.C. The city's location on a peninsula in the Gulf of Tunis and its two good harbors made it an important trading post during much of Tunisia's history.

2) History and Government

Archaeological excavations have revealed that humans lived along the Tunisian coast during the late Stone Age (8000 to 3500 B.C.). Hunters and fishermen, these peoples made stone blades and tools, and evidence suggests that they also raised cattle and cultivated crops. South of the mountains, the regions that are now desert once received plenty of water and supported herds of animals. A culture of hunters and herders flourished until about 2000 B.C., when the savanna began to dry up.

As a result of the change in climate, many of the inhabitants moved north and mixed with the Berber population that lived in the region. Although the origin of the Berbers is unknown, they are thought to have entered North Africa from southwestern Asia around 3000 B.C. Some Berber groups came directly from Asia. Others may have first migrated down the eastern coast of Africa and mingled with Africans before moving northwest to the Mediterranean region.

Carthage

The land that is now Tunisia first appears in written historical records around 1200 B.C., when Phoenician traders from the city of Tyre (in present-day Lebanon) landed on Tunisia's northeastern coast. The Phoenicians equipped the safe harbors along North Africa's shore to service, sup-

When the Phoenicians settled in Carthage, they brought the religious traditions of southwestern Asia with them. Firstborn children were strangled and burned in sacrifice to the god Moloch, and their bones were placed in burial urns.

ply, and shelter their ships. Links in a commercial chain from Tyre to Spain, these ports also connected the Phoenicians with the Berber peoples who lived in the interior. The Phoenicians developed contacts with the Berbers and gave them gifts to gain their cooperation in finding valuable raw materials in the region.

The greatest of the Phoenician colonies was Carthage—or Qart Hadasht, meaning "new town"—which was founded on Tunisia's northeastern coast in 814 B.C. by a Phoenician queen. Thirty miles from Carthage the Phoenicians had previously built the colony of Utica, and these two towns became rivals under the leadership of Tyre. When invaders from Mesopotamia (modern Iraq) overcame Tyre in the sixth century B.C., however, Carthage gained supremacy over all of the Phoenician colonies

Both a commercial and a military port were contained within the harbors at Carthage, and a narrow channel connected them. Naval offices stood on the circular islet in the middle of the harbor, and hidden coves along the shore sheltered 220 warships. The port facilities exhibit the engineering feats of the Carthaginians, who moved over 326,000 cubic yards of earth during construction. Eventually, the Romans would learn both engineering and naval warfare from the Carthaginians.

along the North African coast. Parts of Spain and Italy also fell to the Carthaginians, who threatened to control the entire Mediterranean.

Governed by a merchant oligarchy (a group of a few rulers), the Carthaginians imported the religious, legal, and governmental concepts practiced by the Phoenicians. Two elected suffetes (officials) exercised executive power through a senate made up of respected decision makers. The constitution combined elements of monarchy, aristocracy, and democracy. Settlements along the coast governed themselves but depended on Carthage for military defense and for international diplomacy.

Built on a peninsula in the Gulf of Tunis, Carthage had two excellent harbors. A surrounding wall and a fortress protected the city. The city wall also contained one of the harbors, providing refuge for hundreds of vessels. Although the Carthaginians were more interested in trade than in conquest, they used military power when foreigners threatened their domain.

Such threats came at first from the Greeks, who fought to gain control of the island of Sicily. Until the fifth century B.C. Carthage remained superior during battle by forming an alliance with the Etruscans of central Italy. After Etruscan power declined, however, Carthage experienced its first defeat in 480 B.C., when the Greeks overpowered Carthaginian forces on Sicily. Although the Carthaginians retained part of the island until the third century B.C., they no longer held complete control of southern Mediterranean trade routes.

The Punic Wars

As Rome gained strength and extended its empire throughout Italy in the third century B.C., it also struggled for overseas possessions. The Roman (Latin) term for Phoenician was *Punic*, and Roman expansion began with the Punic Wars waged against Carthage.

Carved from stone, this ship illustrates a type constructed by the Phoenicians in the third century B.C.

Although the Romans had little experience on the seas, they developed a naval power able to meet the Carthaginians on equal terms during the First Punic War (264–241 B.C.). Carthaginian forces led by Hamilcar Barca lost Sicily to the Romans but gained territory in Spain, where Rome had not yet established its influence.

In the Second Punic War (218–201 B.C.) Hamilcar Barca's son Hannibal marched eastward from Spain along the Mediterranean shore and crossed the Alps into Italy. A highly respected leader and military strategist, Hannibal surprised the Romans with his daring maneuvers. Although Hannibal gained success initially, his troops were badly outnumbered and the Romans prevented reinforcements from reaching him. The final blow to the Carthaginians came when the Romans invaded North Africa before Hannibal had returned home. By the war's end Carthage had lost Spain as well as various island possessions.

Although Rome allowed the city of Carthage to govern itself, the Carthaginians eventually rebelled against restrictions imposed by the peace treaty of 201 B.C. The Third—and last—Punic War erupted in 149 B.C. Within three years the Romans had destroyed Carthage, and they eventually became the supreme power in the Western world. Many Carthaginians fled to the interior of present-day Tunisia, where Carthaginian and Berber cultures intermixed in rural North Africa.

Roman Rule

Rome annexed Carthaginian territory and eventually organized it into the province of Proconsular Africa, which was governed by a civilian official (proconsul) appointed by the Roman senate. In 44 B.C. Julius Caesar—supreme ruler of the Roman Empire—ordered the rebuilding of Carthage as the capital of the province. Within two centuries the new Carthage had become

the third most important city in the empire, after Rome and Alexandria, Egypt.

For 400 years Proconsular Africa prospered. Agriculture replaced commerce as the foundation of the economy. Indeed, the province became known as the "granary of Rome," exporting two-thirds of its wheat production, in addition to growing grapes and olives.

By the second century A.D. Christianity —a monotheistic (one-god) religion founded by Jesus of Nazareth—had reached Proconsular Africa. The new faith had arisen in Palestine, a region east of the Mediterranean, after Jesus' death in about A.D. 30. Initially, Christianity served the local North African populations as a form of protest against the Roman Empire, which had not yet adopted the new religion. Although the empire thrived, African peoples received low pay for their labor, and their discontent with Roman rule increased.

During the Second Punic War, Hannibal marched through Spain and France, boldly crossing the Pyrenees Mountains and the Alps before reaching Roman Italy. Along with his forces Hannibal brought several elephants—seen here crossing France's Rhône River on rafts—which he used in battle to break through the enemy line. Despite Hannibal's brilliant military strategies, the Romans eventually defeated him when his supplies and troops began to dwindle.

Photo by Drs. A. A. M. van der Heyden, Naarden, the Netherlands

Numerous remains from the Roman period still stand at Sbeïtla, in central Tunisia. This temple is one of three structures that rise on platforms above a forum (marketplace) and that are surrounded by a high wall.

Vandals and Byzantines

Because Rome faced troubles with its own population, it had little time and few resources to police its African holdings. In A.D. 429 the Vandals, a Germanic people led by King Genseric, crossed Spain into

Photo by Drs. A. A. M. van der Heyden, Naarden, the Netherlands

The arena of the amphitheater at Carthage is now overgrown with grass and wildflowers. During the Roman period, however, human and animal fights and the execution of Christians were held in the arena for public entertainment.

Photo by Drs. A. A. M. van der Heyden, Naarden, the Netherlands

A Roman Catholic cathedral amid the Roman ruins of Carthage attests to the rise of Christianity in the region. By the end of the fourth century A.D., many people in North Africa had converted to the new faith.

North Africa. By 439 Carthage had come under Vandal control. Rather than changing Tunisian society, the Vandals continued Roman institutions. They kept many Roman laws and customs and retained local Roman administrators. Vandal rulers succeeded in stabilizing the region, but they failed to develop their own permanent administrative framework, and the economy declined.

When the Vandal king Hilderic forged an alliance with the Byzantine, or Eastern Roman, Empire to strengthen his rule, Vandal troops overthrew Hilderic. The uprising provided the Byzantine emperor Justinian with an opportunity to attack the Vandal state. In 533 Byzantine troops led by Belisarius landed near Carthage and quickly overcame the Vandals, who had not built up a strong defense system.

Byzantine rulers sought to increase their wealth by restoring the prosperity of earlier Roman rule, a prospect that angered the local Berbers. Attacks from the Berbers forced the Byzantines to stay primarily on the coast. Religious conflicts emerged when various Christian sects did not accept the Christian beliefs held by Byzantine emperors. These conflicts further

Photo by Drs. A. A. M. van der Heyden, Naarden, the Netherlands

The Byzantines created beautiful mosaics from chips of variously colored material. The woman in this mosaic holds an olive branch.

weakened Byzantine control in Africa. In 646 Gregory, the governor of the empire's African province, declared the region's independence.

Disagreements within the Christian community enabled a new force—Islam—to enter the region. Muhammad, a prophet from Saudi Arabia, founded this new monotheistic faith early in the seventh century. Moving from the Arabian Peninsula in southwestern Asia, the Muslims—followers of Islam—gradually extended their realm throughout southwestern Asia and North Africa. The Muslim conquest of the area now known as Tunisia signaled the end of Western influences. As in Phoenician times, Asian peoples once again became the dominant force in the region.

The Muslim Conquest

In 670 Arab Muslims led by Uqba ibn Nafi entered the Roman province of Africa, which they called Ifriqiya in Arabic, and founded the city of Kairouan as a military base in present-day Tunisia. Carthage fell to the Arabs in 693, but the Arabs did not completely overcome Byzantine resistance until they gained naval supremacy on the Mediterranean.

Although much of the Berber population converted to Islam, the people were much slower to adopt Arab ways. Tunisia, along with the rest of the Muslim conquests, came under the control of the Umayyad dynasty (family of rulers). Later, after 750, the Abbasid dynasty ruled Tunisia from Baghdad, Iraq. The caliph (supreme ruler

Courtesy of Embassy of Tunisia

The massive minaret of the Great Mosque at Kairouan rises 115 feet above the ground. Part of a structure built by the Aghlabids in 836, the tower is the oldest existing minaret in the world. From the top a muezzin, or crier, calls Muslims to prayer five times each day.

The Aghlabids built many ribats (Muslim monasteries), such as this one near Tunis. Heavily fortified, they served both military and religious purposes. The stone walls protected inhabitants of the ribat from invading Berber and Christian troops. The ribat also provided a place for holy Muslims—called marabouts—to pray and to study the Koran (Islamic sacred writings).

of Islam) turned local governing over to a succession of emirs (commanders) who were responsible to the central Islamic government.

THE AGHLABIDS

In 800 the Abbasid caliph appointed Ibrahim ibn al-Aghlab as emir of Ifriqiya, and he established a hereditary dynasty known as the Aghlabids. For the next century the Aghlabids ruled the region as an independent state with little connection to the caliph in faraway Iraq. The period became known as a golden age for Ifriqiya, because the region developed a political and cultural identity that was different from the rest of the Islamic world.

At the peak of their rule the Aghlabids conquered Sicily and transformed Kairouan into a religious and cultural center that attracted pilgrims and scholars from all over the Islamic world. The Aghlabids introduced Arabic architecture to Tunisia, building some of the country's finest mosques and many fortified towns. Eventually, however, the Aghlabids fell from power. Partly because the Aghlabids had failed to consider the economic and po-

litical interests of the local Berbers, the Fatimids—a rival North African group—were able to overcome the Aghlabids in 910. The conquerors transferred the capital from Kairouan to Mahdia on Tunisia's eastern coast.

THE FATIMIDS

The Fatimids—who claimed descent from Fatima, a daughter of Muhammad—belonged to Shiite Islam, a sect that opposed the Abbasid caliphate in Baghdad. Shiites believed that only descendants of Muhammad should hold Muslim leadership. The Abbasids, who were of the Sunni sect, elected their leaders. Berbers in Ifriqiya readily adopted Shiism as a means to express their dissatisfaction with the Aghlabids—Sunnis who supported the Abbasid religious leaders. Fatimid armies swept over all of the Maghrib and captured most of Egypt as well, where they eventually established their capital.

Fatimid leadership was harsh and intolerant toward the Berbers, who over the centuries had grown to resent foreign rule. After moving their capital to Cairo, Egypt, in 973, the Fatimids left the governing

23

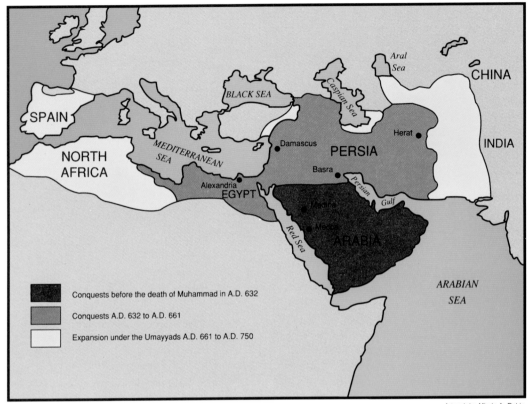

Artwork by Mindy A. Rabin

Armies made up of Muslims conquered Tunisia in the second half of the seventh century. Their realm eventually stretched from Western Europe to India.

of the Maghrib to Buluggin ibn Ziri. He became the first leader of the Zirid dynasty.

Gradually, the Fatimids turned their attention toward acquiring new territory, and they lost interest in North Africa. In their place the Zirids, who were Berbers, established a North African Muslim state (with headquarters in Kairouan) dedicated to the interests of the Berber majority.

Berber Dynasties

For the next six centuries, from 973 to 1575, Berber rulers controlled Ifriqiya. The Berber reign represented a welcome change from the foreign domination that had occurred since the days of the Phoenicians. But the Berber dynasties faced other problems.

THE ZIRIDS

The Fatimids did not pose a major threat to Zirid control. Indeed, even when the Zirids renounced Shiism in favor of Sunni Muslim practices, the Fatimids did not try to convert them back to Shiism. Loss of Fatimid influence, however, had a serious economic impact on Ifriqiya. Caravan routes that had connected the interior with the Mediterranean lost the traffic they had received from Fatimid trade.

Furthermore, when the Berbers returned to Sunni beliefs, the Fatimids pushed nomadic Bedouin—a wandering Arab people who depended on herding for their livelihood—from Egypt into the Maghrib. The Zirid's economic problems consequently increased, because the newly arrived Bedouin disrupted agriculture with their herds. Fertile land became pasture, which forced many Berber farmers to join the Bedouin as shepherds.

In an attempt to improve the economy, the Zirids turned to the sea in the hope of reviving Mediterranean trade. But their efforts came too late, because European Christians were already extending their commercial activities into the central Mediterranean. Unable to meet outside threats or to improve its economy, the Zirid dynasty slowly crumbled, and Christian and Muslim rivals divided the spoils.

THE ALMOHADS

With the decline of the Zirids, the Almohads (another Berber dynasty) pushed into Ifriqiya from Morocco in the western Maghrib. By 1160 the Almohads had eliminated Christian strongholds in Ifriqiya, adding them to the Almohad realm. The Almohad acquisitions represented the first and last unified North African empire.

The local population of Ifriqiya initially was pleased to have the Almohads rescue them from the threat of Christian domination. But they soon began to fear losing their independence. The Almohads, however, were unable to maintain order in all of North Africa and southern Spain, which also came under their control. They left the governing of Ifriqiya to the Hafsid family,

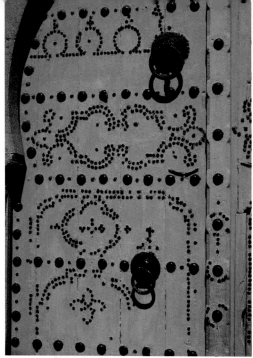

Blue doors with ironwork characterize the buildings of Sidi Bou Said, a Muslim town named after its thirteenth-century patron, Abou Said al-Baji.

which gained supremacy in Ifriqiya as Almohad authority weakened.

THE HAFSIDS

Hafsid leaders adopted the titles of caliph and sultan and claimed to be the legitimate successors of the Almohads. In 1228 Abu Zakariya al-Hafs took power

Berbers from Tunisia's interior dug more than 20 feet under the ground to build homes that were cool despite the Saharan heat. Steps or earthen ramps led down to an open courtyard, off which were small sleeping quarters and storerooms. The local inhabitants of Matmata continue to live in these dwellings.

Carpets that illustrate Berber, Persian, and Turkish designs have been sold by Tunisian traders for centuries. The industry is centered in Kairouan, where there is a rug market and an annual rug fair.

and moved the capital of Ifriqiya from Kairouan to Tunis, and Ifriqiya became known as Tunisia. As a result of the move, coastal cities became more important than inland centers in political and economic affairs. Hafsid sultans encouraged trade with Europe and exchanged ambassadors with countries as far away as Norway.

The shared traditions of Spain and the Maghrib—known as Moorish culture—

that arose under the Almohads reached Tunisia during the Hafsid reign, and Tunis became a center of Islamic learning and arts. Despite their scholastic and artistic achievements, however, the Hafsids lost power as internal rivals and foreign groups—including pirates and Christian crusaders—threatened Hafsid stability. Nevertheless, the Hafsid era continued for 300 years, during which Tunisia forged a distinctive identity as a commercial, diplomatic, and artistic center within the Islamic world.

The Ottoman Empire

By the early sixteenth century the Ottoman Turks had entered the competition for control of Mediterranean lands and trade routes. For the next 50 years authority over Tunis shifted among the Hafsids, the Spanish, and the Turks. In 1575 an army of Turkish ships and 40,000 troops forced the Spanish out of Tunis and carried the last of the Hafsids to Istanbul, the Ottoman capital in Turkey.

In 1587 Turkish rulers divided the Maghrib into three regencies (administrative units). Tunis became the seat of one regency, headed by a pasha (governor). The pasha's role, however, was largely ceremonial, and Turkish troops—called Janissaries —stationed in Tunisia held the real power.

PIRACY

While the Janissaries maintained order and collected taxes in Tunisia, pirates of the Barbary States (Morocco, Algiers, and Tripoli) provided the rulers with a steady income from raids and from wars waged at sea against Spain. The Turks considered piracy a business and planned it as part of their naval strategy in the Mediterranean. Pirate captains raided ships and European coastal towns. They captured hostages and held them for ransom or sold them at slave markets.

Mutinies and coups were frequent, and the Janissaries were loyal to whoever paid them regularly. European maritime powers began to pay tribute to the rulers of Tunis and the other Barbary States to insure themselves against attacks on their shipping. In 1799 the United States signed a treaty with Tunisia to protect North American shipping, and in 1818 a British-French fleet enforced a treaty that made

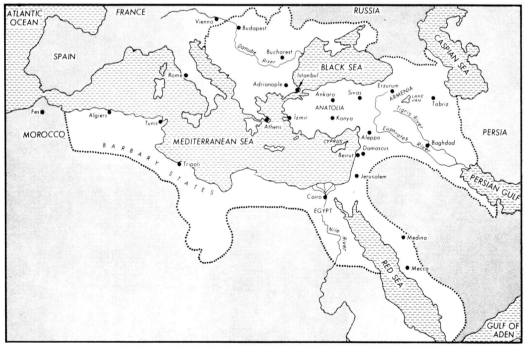

By the middle of the seventeenth century, the Ottoman Empire included all of the Middle East, much of the North African coast, and most of Eastern Europe. Map taken from *The Area Handbook for the Republic of Turkey,* 1973.

A colorful Turkish painting depicts Ottoman forces attacking the port at Tunis in 1575.

A military parade shows the excellent training that made Ottoman troops hard to defeat in battle.

From the sixteenth to the early nineteenth centuries piracy flourished in the Mediterranean. The booty and slaves captured in raids supported Muslim rulers along the Barbary Coast. In 1804 the U.S. Navy attempted to stop attacks on U.S. shipping in the Battle of Tripoli.

it illegal to arm pirates or to take Christians as slaves in the Barbary States.

THE HUSAYNIDS

In 1705 Husayn ibn Ali—whose descendants held the throne until 1957—founded the Husaynid dynasty of Tunisia and gave himself the title of bey, or king. The Husaynids cultivated connections with the Ottoman Empire to increase Turkish acceptance of them. At the same time, however, they maintained enough distance to remain independent. Strong Husaynid rulers ensured their stability by yielding to the demands of the Janissaries while cultivating local Arab support to offset the power of the Janissaries. Several of the beys, however, developed a habit of using government money for personal luxuries, which seriously disrupted Tunisia's economy.

In 1837 the Husaynid leader Ahmad Bey came to power and initiated reforms to improve the failing economy. Ahmad also decided to draft Tunisians for military service, promoting the idea of a homeland defended by its citizens rather than by a small group of outsiders. The bey hoped that this move would inspire his subjects with a greater sense of loyalty and concern for the state's future. Ahmad's reform programs were expensive, however, and his personal spending habits were careless. As a result, he nearly bankrupted the country.

During the nineteenth century, in the face of economic deterioration, the beys borrowed money from European creditors. France, Italy, and Great Britain—who each wanted to take over North Africa—provided Tunisia with loans. In 1868 the International Financial Commission (IFC) took charge of reorganizing Tunisia's finances. The commission's members included one Tunisian—Khayr al-Din—as well as French, British, and Italian representatives.

Khayr al-Din

In 1873 Khayr al-Din became Tunisia's prime minister, replacing Mustafa Khaznadar. In contrast to the corrupt Khaznadar, whom Tunisians finally succeeded in removing from office after 36 years, Khayr al-Din was known as a reform leader and nationalist. He had formulated the Constitution of 1861—the first written constitution in the Islamic world. Among other changes, the document created a secular (nonreligious) supreme court to review decisions by the sharia (Islamic law) courts.

A bold document within Muslim countries, the constitution had many opponents. Rural Tunisians, for example, felt that the new laws stripped them of their local authority and freedom. Popular resentment erupted in a rebellion that forced the government to suspend the constitution in 1864. The experience left Khayr al-Din still confident but more realistic about his goals for Tunisia.

Cooperating with the IFC, Khayr al-Din introduced reforms as prime minister that greatly improved Tunisia's finances. But European financial leaders prevented other changes, such as land reform, that would have hurt their own interests while improving conditions for the local population.

Although the Europeans at first were pleased with Khayr al-Din's initiatives, they cooled toward him when his success threatened their own concerns. Pressure from the French brought about Khayr al-Din's dismissal from office in 1877. He was replaced by an ineffective leader who compounded Tunisia's problems.

The French Protectorate

At the Berlin Conference in the late nineteenth century, the European powers—which had been competing for control of various parts of Africa for several decades—divided the African continent among themselves. France received the right to control Tunisia's affairs and decided to occupy the country at the earliest opportunity.

In 1881 a French army entered Tunisia from French-ruled Algeria, claiming to be in pursuit of a group of Tunisians who had crossed the Algerian border. The French wanted to ensure their Tunisian holdings and to thwart Italians who wanted the

A nineteenth-century painting illustrates the Tunisian and French cavalries engaged in battle during the French invasion of 1881.

region. The invaders forced the bey to sign the Bardo Treaty, which made Tunisia a French protectorate.

Although the bey retained his position, a French resident-general governed the country. The French brought Western technology to Tunisia, building roads and railways, improving ports, and introducing modern medical services. They seized the best agricultural land and handed it over to French settlers. The French also exploited the region's mineral reserves.

Nationalist Movements

In response to French rule, vigorous nationalist movements arose among a small, educated segment of Tunisians. For several decades French authorities successfully suppressed these groups. The Destour (Constitution) party, however, gained momentum. Founded in 1920, this group wanted to reinstate the Constitution of 1861 and to initiate extensive democratic reforms. Promising not to use violence, the party became a voice for Tunisian discontent in the 1920s by organizing labor strikes and demonstrations. When party member Habib Bourguiba publicly called for Tunisian independence in 1933, the French resident-general ordered the party to disband.

A young intellectual who had joined the Destour party when he returned from law school in France, Bourguiba was distressed at how little progress the party had made in his absence. He founded the Neo-Destour (New Constitution) party in 1934 with the goal of appealing more to Tunisia's general population. For the next several years, Bourguiba alternated between leading the Neo-Destour party and living either in exile from Tunisia or in prison because of his political activities.

World War II

After Nazi Germany occupied France in 1940, French authorities in Tunisia coop-

Courtesy of Agency for International Development

A military cemetery and memorial in Tunisia commemorates soldiers who died while fighting in North Africa during World War II.

erated with the pro-German government in Vichy, France. Most Tunisians preferred Vichy rule to Italian control exercised from neighboring Libya, and they temporarily set aside their quest for independence to support Vichy France in the war.

Tunisia was the battleground for important military operations during the war. When Allied (anti-Nazi) forces landed in Algiers and Morocco in November 1942, Germany entered northern Tunisia to resist the Allied advance. After several months of fighting, the Allied forces cornered the Germans on the Cape Bon Peninsula. The surrender, which occurred in May 1943, marked the final defeat of the Axis (German-allied) powers in North Africa, and Tunisia came under the control of the Free French (the French under Charles de Gaulle, who resisted the Germans).

Independence

After World War II Tunisia's struggle for independence regained momentum. By the 1950s popular demonstrations had steadily increased, and the French had

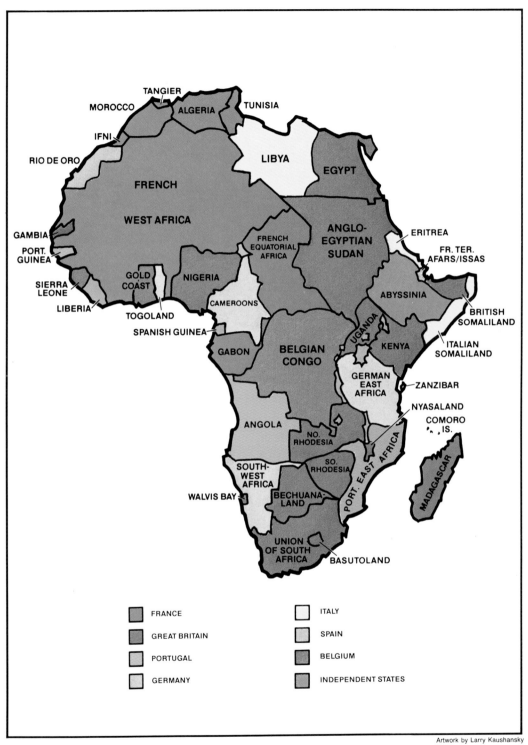

France: FRANCE
Great Britain: GREAT BRITAIN
Portugal: PORTUGAL
Germany: GERMANY
Italy: ITALY
Spain: SPAIN
Belgium: BELGIUM
Independent States: INDEPENDENT STATES

Artwork by Larry Kaushansky

By the late nineteenth century, the Europeans had carved the African continent into areas of influence. Present-day Tunisia was a French protectorate from 1881 to 1956. Map information taken from *The Anchor Atlas of World History*, 1978.

Tunisian governmental officials—including Habib Bourguiba *(middle)*—salute the Tunisian flag shortly after their country gained independence.

difficulty maintaining order. In July 1954 they promised Tunisians full internal self-rule—but not independence—hoping that this measure would satisfy Tunisians. Although some Neo-Destour members opposed the French offer for internal autonomy, Bourguiba accepted it as a stepping stone, recognizing that each small gain would eventually lead to complete independence.

Tunisia achieved full independence on March 20, 1956, when the French ended the Bardo Treaty of 1881 and recognized Tunisia as a constitutional monarchy ruled by the bey of Tunis. The Neo-Destour party won a majority of the seats in the first national legislative elections, and Bourguiba was elected president of the Tunisian national assembly. Assembly members adopted a constitution, and in 1957 they deposed the last Husaynid bey, proclaimed Tunisia a republic, and elected Bourguiba president of Tunisia. Bourguiba was reelected in 1959, 1964, and 1969. Under a special law passed in 1975 he was named president for life.

The New Republic

After gaining independence, Bourguiba and his associates enacted a program of social change, hoping to show Tunisians the value of modernity and progress. But Bourguiba also was aware that most Tunisians had a more traditional perspective than the one he and other Western-educated officials had.

Consequently, he assured religious conservatives that he would not attack Islam. Instead, he would examine Islamic

33

Rising prominently above a government building, the flag of Tunisia dates from 1835 and reflects the country's Ottoman past. The red field, the white disk—which represents the sun—the star, and the crescent were symbols of the Ottoman Empire. For many Arab countries, red also stood for their resistance to Turkish rule. The crescent moon, which Arabs believe brings good luck, and the five-pointed star are also ancient Islamic symbols.

institutions and adapt them to the twentieth century. To prove that his sympathies lay with Muslims, he declared Islam the state religion. But the Neo-Destour party also liberalized traditional Islamic practices that affected education, medical services, and the status of women. This drive for social reform inspired similar trends in other Arab countries.

During the early years of independence, tensions grew between France and Tunisia over the presence of French troops still stationed at the naval base in Bizerte. The dispute erupted into violence in 1961. In the following year the French finally agreed to evacuate their forces.

Conflicts between the two nations escalated again in 1964, however, when Tunisia nationalized (converted to government ownership) all foreign-owned lands—most of which were held by the French. In response, France canceled all financial assistance to Tunisia, leaving the country in a serious economic crisis. The Tunisian decision to nationalize signaled a greater emphasis on socialism (government control of businesses and services). Later that year the Neo-Destour party changed its name to the Socialist Destour party (PSD).

Inter-Arab Relations

Tunisia's relations with other Arab nations have alternated between friendly and tense. At times Tunisia's views have differed widely from those of other Arab states. During the 1950s and 1960s Bourguiba clashed with Egypt's president Gamal Abdel Nasser, who enthusiastically supported Arab unity and promoted Arab actions against Israel. A nation on the eastern shore of the Mediterranean, Israel had been created in 1948 to provide a national home for the Jewish people. The new state and the influx of Jewish immigrants displaced many Palestinian Arabs.

Although Bourguiba supported the cause of the Palestinians, he felt they should achieve the return of their homeland peacefully and gradually, as he had done to gain independence for Tunisians. To demonstrate his disapproval of Arab policies, particularly those against Israel, Bourguiba delayed allowing Tunisia to join the Arab League. This organization was formed in 1945 by the heads of Arab states to strengthen Arab unity and to address Arab concerns. For several years after finally joining the league in 1958, Tunisia participated only minimally in the organization.

Popular sentiments in Tunisia, however, often were much more closely allied with the rest of the Arab world. Bourguiba's ill health in the early 1970s gave other Tunisian officials the opportunity to take more power. Those who wanted to build strong Arab ties influenced foreign policy and improved Tunisia's standing in the region.

When the Arab world rejected Egypt for signing a peace treaty with Israel in 1979, the Arab League moved its headquarters from Cairo to Tunis. Many Tunisians filled key positions in the league, and Tunisia's influence on Arab affairs greatly increased. In 1982 Israel invaded Beirut, Lebanon,

From the steps of a pavilion, an Arab in traditional clothing views the splendor of the mausoleum (above-ground tomb) built for President Habib Bourguiba during his lifetime.

and forced the Palestine Liberation Organization (PLO)—the representative group of the Palestinian people—to withdraw. The PLO relocated its headquarters to Tunis.

Because it has become a center for Arab affairs, Tunisia has received economic aid from oil-rich Middle Eastern countries. But its new status has made Tunis a target for Israeli retaliation. In 1985 Israeli jets bombed the PLO headquarters near Tunis.

Domestic Unrest

During the late 1970s and the 1980s, discontent increased among Tunisians. Because the PSD had been the only legal political party in Tunisia since the mid-1960s, critics of Bourguiba's regime had little impact on government policies. The country faced severe economic problems —including a high unemployment rate— and students and workers protested frequently. Labor riots broke out during a general strike in 1978.

The 1978 riots forced officials to consider opposing viewpoints. In 1979 the PSD's leaders recognized that they had to open up the government to accommodate different perspectives. In 1981 they legalized the Tunisian Communist party. Several other parties, however, including the conservative Islamic Tendency movement, still lacked official recognition.

Severe riots broke out again in 1984 in response to the government's decision to double the price of bread. The measure in itself could not have corrected the economy, and the riots ended only when Bourguiba returned the price to its normal level.

During the riots of 1978 President Bourguiba called a state of emergency and enforced a curfew from sunset to sunrise. This tank was positioned on guard outside the parliamentary building *(right)* and the Ministry of Finance *(left)* to control striking workers who were protesting against price increases and low wages.

For over half a century Habib Bourguiba *(right)* guided Tunisia through independence and modernization. His increasingly repressive style of leadership, however, led to his downfall in 1987 to Zine al-Abidine ben Ali.

Unrest continued during the mid-1980s, and Bourguiba tightened his control over the government by further limiting opposition. The aging president—who turned 84 in 1987—began to reshuffle his government in 1986, dismissing longtime aides, including Prime Minister Mohammed Mzali, Bourguiba's handpicked successor. His actions seemed to reflect his fear of political liberalization and democratic reforms.

On November 7, 1987, Prime Minister Zine al-Abidine ben Ali took control of the government in a nonviolent coup. He announced that Bourguiba, whose health had been failing for several years, was too ill to govern any longer. Ben Ali stressed the need for democratic reforms and created commissions to draft laws allowing independent political parties, constitutional changes, and greater freedom of the press. Although Tunisians generally favored the changes during the first months after the takeover, the pro-Western ben Ali faces challenges from Muslim fundamentalists (conservatives), who prefer Islam-based policies.

Government Structure

When Tunisia adopted the Constitution of 1959, it became a republic headed by a president. The president, who also serves as commander in chief of the army, is elected for a five-year term and may run for reelection an unlimited number of times. The chief executive appoints a cabinet, headed by a prime minister, to assist in carrying out executive policy. The prime minister succeeds the president in case of death or disability.

The 125-member unicameral (one-house) national assembly also is elected for five-year terms. All Tunisians over the age of 19 who have been citizens for five years may vote. The legislature meets twice a year, with each session lasting no longer than three months.

The Constitution of 1959 replaced religious courts with civil tribunals. At the bottom of the judicial ladder are cantonal, or local, courts. More important cases go to courts of first instance. Courts of appeal hear cases that are being retried. At the top of the judicial system is the final outlet for appeals, the court of cassation.

Tunisia is divided into 23 governorates, or states, for the local administration of government. Governors, who are appointed by the president, each head their own local region.

A young Tunisian woman who lives near Kairouan displays a traditional costume worn in the region.

3) The People

Tunisians are almost entirely a mixture of Berber and Arab peoples. Although Tunisians have accepted the customs, language, religion, and traditions of the Arabs as their own, they generally consider themselves more Tunisian than Arab. Perhaps this is one reason why the country has remained stable since gaining independence—Tunisians tend to concentrate more on their own national unity than on regional Arab unity.

In 1988 an estimated 7.7 million people lived in Tunisia, making it one of the most densely populated countries in North Africa. Tunisia's average of 103 people per square mile is extremely high for a desert country. In the northern third of the land, the density is even higher, but in the south, the number drops to less than 10 people per square mile. A majority of the population is young, with 40 percent of the people under 15 years of age.

Less than 1 percent of Tunisia's population is European. A small percentage of black Tunisians, whose ancestors were brought in as slaves from Africa's interior before the abolition of the slave trade in 1841, also make up part of the population.

The type of work Tunisians do is likely to be determined by the area of the country they live in. In the north, many people are farmers, fishermen, and office or factory workers. The eastern coast is also an important agricultural area, and tree farming employs the highest number of people in that region. The semi-arid and desert south belongs mostly to miners and to Bedouin herders.

Religion

Islam is the state religion in Tunisia. Although 99 percent of all Tunisians practice Islam, they are tolerant of other faiths. The word *Islam* means submission to the will of God, whose laws were revealed to Muhammad and were recorded in the Koran (the Islamic holy book). Muslims believe that there is only one God, whose name is Allah. Muhammad, who founded the religion in the seventh century A.D., is considered an earthly prophet rather than a divine being. Tunisians who have adopted Western attitudes consider the teachings of Muhammad less important than do other Tunisians and Muslims from the rest of the Arab world.

Devout Muslims pray five times a day, kneeling on the ground wherever they may be at prayer time. They say part of the prayer with their heads touching the ground while they face toward the holy city of Mecca in Saudi Arabia. Friday is a sacred day to Muslims, and in the

Courtesy of Tunisian National Tourist Office, Tunis

A stark white mosque stands out amid the stone buildings and caves on the rocky slopes of Chenini, a Berber town in the Ksour Mountains of the desert south. Mosques are a common feature in Tunisia, where almost everyone follows Islam.

Named after its thirteenth-century patron, Abou Said al-Baji, the town of Sidi Bou Said draws Muslim pilgrims from all over the country. Situated on the slopes of a hill that overlooks the Gulf of Tunis, Sidi Bou Said also attracts artists, writers, and vacationers.

afternoon they usually go to the mosque for prayers. Although in many Islamic countries only Muslims are welcome at mosques, Tunisian mosques are open to all visitors except at prayer time.

Muslims must try to make a pilgrimage to Mecca—a 2,000-mile journey for Tunisians—once during their lives. The country's own holy city of Kairouan is also a place of pilgrimage, however, and for Tunisian Muslims who cannot go to Mecca, seven trips to Kairouan equal one journey to Mecca. In addition, many towns in Tunisia have a patron religious leader. The word *sidi* is an African Muslim title of respect, and the towns of Sidi Bou Said, Sidi Mechrig, and Sidi Daoud are named after local holy men. Along Tunisia's roadways—especially those along the eastern coast—small, whitewashed shrines contain relics of saints.

Just as a mosque usually dominates the old section of each town, the new section often contains a Catholic church constructed by the French. In addition, several Italian communities in the north have built their own Catholic churches. Less than 1 percent of the population is Christian, and Jews also account for less than 1 percent of the people.

Language

Muslim invaders brought the Arabic language to Tunisia in the seventh century. Since then it has become the official language of Tunisians. Written from right to left, Arabic script is the same for all Arabic-speakers from Morocco to Iraq. But Arabic is spoken with a variety of accents, and even within the borders of Tunisia pronunciation is not always the same. The

Independent Picture Service

Although very few Tunisians still speak the Berber language, lighter skin and darker clothes generally differentiate Berber descendants from their Arab neighbors.

Tunisian government uses state-owned television and radio broadcasting services to help standardize the country's spoken Arabic.

Only about 1 percent of all Tunisians still speak the region's native Berber tongue as a first language. Although some Tunisians still perform ancient Berber folk songs, few people understand them. French, which served as the official language when Tunisia was a protectorate, remains important in government and social circles, and nearly half the population speaks it as a second language. French is taught in all schools, and two of Tunis's four daily newspapers are published in French.

Education

Although public education is free and is available to all Tunisians, children are not required to attend classes. Nevertheless, with a national literacy rate of about 46 percent in 1985, the government has dedicated itself to improving the educational system. Indeed, the government devotes as much as 25 to 30 percent of its budget to education.

Primary and secondary schools hold classes six days a week for nine months of the year. Primary schools in some areas operate double shifts because of a shortage of facilities. The first two years of education are taught in Arabic, but thereafter students begin to learn French. Science, mathematics, and technical courses are generally taught in French. The University of Tunis is the country's major institution of higher learning.

The government views education as a vital means to further the nation's social

Tunisian high school students answer questions during an economics class. Because the government is dedicated to improving educational opportunities in Tunisia, it devotes over one-quarter of the national budget to education.

Independent Picture Service

41

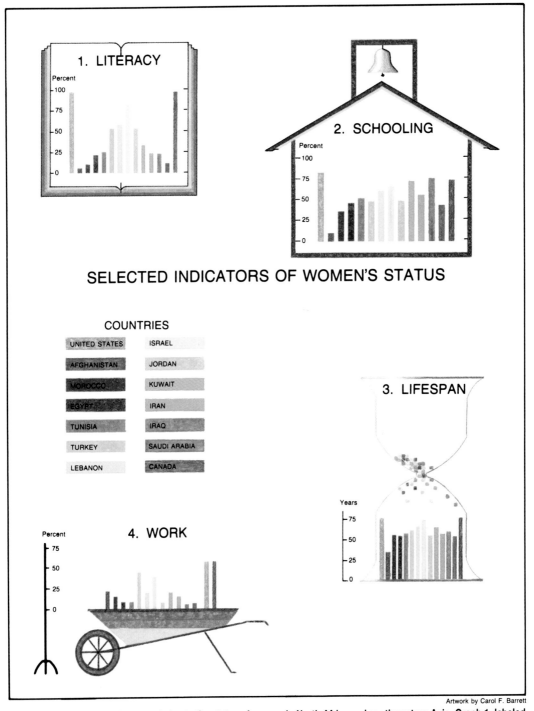

SELECTED INDICATORS OF WOMEN'S STATUS

1. LITERACY

2. SCHOOLING

3. LIFESPAN

4. WORK

COUNTRIES

UNITED STATES
AFGHANISTAN
MOROCCO
EGYPT
TUNISIA
TURKEY
LEBANON

ISRAEL
JORDAN
KUWAIT
IRAN
IRAQ
SAUDI ARABIA
CANADA

Artwork by Carol F. Barrett

Depicted in this chart are factors relating to the status of women in North Africa and southwestern Asia. Graph 1, labeled Literacy, shows the percentage of adult women who can read and write. Graph 2 illustrates the proportion of school-aged girls who actually attend elementary and secondary schools. Graph 3 depicts the life expectancy of female babies at birth. Graph 4 shows the percentage of women in the income-producing work force. Data taken from *Women in the World: An International Atlas,* 1986 and from *Women . . . A World Survey,* 1985.

and economic development. Tunisian citizens also recognize the value of education to improve their individual social and economic status, and school enrollments have increased dramatically since the country gained independence. Unfortunately, employment opportunities have not increased at the same rate, and many young people have been unable to find jobs that match their level of education. Some have found no employment at all. The situation created unrest in the 1970s and 1980s among those who could not achieve the economic gains they thought an education would guarantee.

The Status of Women

Women have historically been somewhat freer in Tunisia than they have been in most Muslim countries. Yet until the mid-twentieth century Tunisian women were restricted to the home and were required to play a subordinate role to men.

Husbands held unquestioned positions of power. In their absence, they delegated authority to the oldest or best-educated son rather than to a wife.

Members of the Neo-Destour party began to question the status of women in Tunisian society during the first half of the twentieth century. The party believed that Tunisia's human resources could be better used by giving women an equal position alongside men. Since gaining independence, the Tunisian government established equal rights for all women, despite the traditional roles followed in Islamic societies.

Women received full citizenship with the right to vote in 1956. The Personal Status Code of 1956 banned polygamy (the practice of a man having more than one wife), required the consent of women in marriage contracts, and raised minimum ages for marriage. The code also gave women the right to marry non-Muslims and to divorce their husbands, and it increased their

A wedding party lines up at a traditional ceremony in southern Tunisia. Although child marriage was once a common practice, in 1964 the legal age for marriage was raised to 17 for females and 20 for males.

Although many Tunisian women wear Western clothing, the rise of conservative Islamic ideals in the 1980s has encouraged some women to return to traditional styles of dress, including the veil.

share of inheritances, which traditionally had gone solely to men.

These new laws, however, could not raise the status of women immediately. Even some women, particularly those of the older generation, opposed such changes. Educated and urban women were the first to exercise their new rights. Many of them followed the government's urging to give up traditional clothing—including a veil that covered the head and face—in favor of Western dress. By 1987 women filled 5 percent of the seats in the national assembly, and 7 percent had entered the labor force.

Tunisian parents continue to encourage sons more than daughters to develop modern attitudes and goals. School enrollment and literacy rates among females have improved, but they still lag behind those of males. The figures, however, are better than they are in other North African countries. The rise of Muslim fundamentalism in the late twentieth century has encouraged Tunisian women to resume traditional practices. Nevertheless, women who choose to maintain a Westernized lifestyle still have government support.

Health

Tunisia's health-care system suffered a severe setback after independence in 1956, when many of the country's European physicians left. Most of those who remained lived in or near Tunis. Since then the government has slowly expanded its facilities and trained Tunisian medical personnel.

Urban Tunisian women, such as these trainees in air traffic control, have found it easier to give up their traditional role than rural women have, in part because education and professions are more readily available to city dwellers.

A man at a Tunisian refreshment stand offers a selection of bottled drinks and freshly squeezed fruit juices to quench the thirst of passersby.

Since 1971 medical students have been required to take training in preventive care. By the late 1970s diseases such as smallpox, typhoid, diphtheria, polio, and typhus had been brought under control. Improvements in the health-care system have helped to reduce the infant mortality rate by half since independence. By 1988 an average of 71 babies out of every 1,000 live births died before their first birthday. Although this rate is still high by Western standards, it is the lowest in North Africa. The life expectancy of 63 years is also the longest in North Africa, and it has increased from 46 years in 1956.

To curb the growth rate of the population, the government began a family-planning program in 1964 to educate women in the use of birth control. The government also legalized abortion in 1973, though it stated that it believed abortion was not an acceptable long-term solution to overpopulation.

The family-planning program was the first of its kind in Africa, and the suggestion that Tunisians would benefit from having smaller families seriously challenged traditional views. Nevertheless, many educated individuals and those who lived in cities adopted the new policy. Forty-one percent of the married women of childbearing age now use some form of birth control. This figure is significantly higher than it is in the rest of Africa. By 1988 authorities estimated Tunisia's population would double in 31 years, which means the population is growing at a slower rate than it has in the past.

Food

Tunisian cooking, which is hearty and spicy, shows French and Italian influences.

A typical North African food, however, is couscous. To make this dish, semolina (a by-product of hard wheat) is sprinkled with oil and water, rolled into tiny morsels, steamed, and then covered with a thick, spicy tomato sauce. The sauce may contain fish, beef, mutton, or vegetables. Italian immigrants have introduced pasta, which Tunisians often serve with couscous sauce. Tunisians sprinkle *harissa*—a condiment of ground red pepper, garlic, salt, and oil— on almost everything they eat.

Charchouka is a simple dish of pimientos, tomatoes, and eggs cooked in butter or olive oil. Its popularity has gained it the name *salade tunisienne*. Tunisians prepare their own version of a French crepe—called a *brik*—which they stuff with meat, fish, eggs, or spinach and fry in oil. *Bouga*, made with lemons, is the country's national soft drink. Tunisians often mix it with wine to make a refreshing drink that combines two products from the country's expanding consumer industries. Mint tea and Turkish coffee are also popular beverages.

Shoppers choose from a wide array of spices at a market on Jerba Island. Tunisian cooks use a variety of seasonings to flavor their dishes.

While a young girl looks on, this woman carefully shapes Tunisian cakes, a crackerlike snack.

At a market in Nabeul, a coastal town near Hammamet, a vendor sets up long trays of bread for sale.

A fluted dome—a common feature of Tunisian architecture—tops a shrine to a Muslim holy man. Stones and marble that date from the Byzantine era form the rest of the structure.

Independent Picture Service

Architecture and the Arts

Unlike the box-shaped houses that many Tunisians occupy, mosques, public buildings, shrines, and the homes of wealthy Tunisians often display the finer details of Arabic architecture. Domes, arches, and minarets (towers) are the features Tunisian architects use in their large-scale designs.

Buildings that date from the period of Islamic rule frequently use elements of both

Independent Picture Service

Mosaics and delicate stone carvings often adorn the interior of religious and public buildings, such as this palace outside Tunis.

Independent Picture Service

Intricately patterned pottery designed in Nabeul keeps alive the artistic styles from ancient civilizations. Carthaginian, Berber, Roman, Byzantine, and Islamic patterns have influenced the work of Tunisian artists and craftspeople.

Independent Picture Service

A wood-carver in Sfax teaches his son skills that have been handed on for generations.

Roman and Arabic styles. For example, Roman marble columns may serve as supports in a mosque. Some of the country's mosques are interesting from the exterior, but the greatest artistic interest of most of them lies in the fine mosaics and carvings that decorate the interior.

A government agency promotes Tunisia's traditional handicrafts. Leather, clay, brass, wood, wrought iron, and wool are the main media for Tunisian craftspeople. Villages tend to specialize in a particular item, and an expert on Tunisian art can tell at a glance which village produced a particular wallet, carved box, blanket, or pair of shoes.

Twentieth-century Tunisian artists and writers have begun to develop their own national style, though they disagree about what the characteristics of this style should be. Some artists from the countryside have kept their Berber traditions alive. Others focus on the Arab-Islamic heritage, which has been the dominant influence in the region. Western styles have affected the work of still others, who analyze European values and the role of those values in Tunisian society.

Independent Picture Service

At Guellala, a potter's colony on Jerba Island, this man carefully sculpts a terra-cotta (fired clay) vase on his potter's wheel. The finished product will have a distinctive, reddish brown color.

49

Divers prepare for a descent at Tabarka. Hemmed in by mountains and the sea, the port town is a center for coral fishing and for the processing and export of cork oak. At one time, Tabarka also served as a pirate haunt.

Tunisian folk dancers entertain visitors at Monastir, along the southern shores of the Gulf of Hammamet. In addition to being a coastal resort, Monastir has a history that stretches back to the time of the Phoenicians. The town was especially important after the eleventh century, when it replaced Kairouan as Tunisia's holy city and center of pilgrimage.

Weavers on Jerba Island produce mats both for local use and for export. The Tunisian government encourages Tunisians to keep traditional arts and crafts alive – a policy that not only protects part of the country's heritage but also earns needed foreign exchange.

4) The Economy

The standard of living for Tunisia's people has risen slowly but steadily since the republic was founded in 1957. Although a major discovery of oil could solve many of the country's economic problems, intensive drilling has produced limited results. Instead, the government has sought prosperity using resources that are available —agriculture, phosphates, tourism, light industry, and small quantities of oil, natural gas, and coal. This variety of activities and products has kept Tunisia's economy more stable than that of nations that depend heavily on one source of income.

Nevertheless, Tunisia has had problems with inflation and unemployment. Strikes and protests urging the government to raise wages and to create more jobs broke out in the 1970s and 1980s. Although the government experimented with state ownership of the nation's businesses in the 1960s, since then officials have encouraged both local and foreign private investment to help stimulate the economy.

Agriculture

Tunisia may have less money than Arab countries that have huge petroleum reserves, but it is fortunate to have the ability to grow its own food. The success of Tunisian farming, however, is unpredictable, because rainfall in any area except the far north can vary greatly from year to year. A drought in 1985 and 1986, for example, drastically reduced the harvest.

The dry, sandy soil along the coast between Sousse and Sfax is ideal for the cultivation of olives. Olive oil, which is pressed from the olives, is one of Tunisia's main agricultural exports.

The rainy north is capable of producing a variety of crops throughout the year, and the middle of the country can support crops during the cool, moist winter. In the south, however, only oases can be used for agricultural purposes. The Sahel receives varying amounts of moisture—in some years crops grow well in the region, and in other years the same crops will be in short supply.

The products that farmers can raise in a given region of the country depend almost entirely on the amount of water that the area receives. Grapes, for example, need a large quantity of moisture, so they grow only on the damp slopes of the north. Alfa grass and olives, which require only limited amounts of rain, grow well in the steppes. Dates thrive on the southern oases, and sheep and goats graze on the grasses of the desert and the steppes. Livestock raising has long been a way of life among nomadic groups. Overgrazing of herds, however, has depleted Tunisia's forests as well as its sparsely vegetated areas.

MAJOR CROPS

Wheat and barley are Tunisia's most important crops, although the government has tried with some success to diversify planting. As much as one-fourth of all farmland produces wheat, barley, and other cereals, which grow in the north on small, privately owned farms. Vegetables, olives, grapes, and other fruits also thrive in the north.

While still using an age-old method for working the land, this man and his camel are able to remove weeds and grass from the ground more easily with a new steel tool rather than with a traditional wooden plow.

The production of olives and olive oil occurs more often farther south, along the eastern coast. Olives are the major crop of the Sahel and are second in importance after cereals. Olive groves completely dominate the landscape as far as 50 miles inland. Cooperatives or the state own most of the huge plantations. The olive has been called Tunisia's gold because it grows well in areas where most other crops would fail without extensive irrigation.

Dates, the third most important agricultural product, flourish in the few areas of watered, fertile soil around oases in the south. Local village governments, which own the land in these fertile areas, sometimes divide the land into tiny plots and lease them to individual planters.

AGRICULTURAL DEVELOPMENT

Although it encourages private business and independent farming, the Tunisian government takes part in all aspects of agricultural planning. Governmental influence has increased productivity and diversity and has greatly decreased foreign-owned plantations.

One of the state's most ambitious efforts has been the Medjerda project—a plan to turn the Medjerda River Valley into one of the most heavily cultivated areas in Africa. Irrigation, flood and erosion control, and artificial drainage have helped to promote high-yield, cooperative farms. The government directs planting and crop rotation to ensure continued productivity. It also encourages the planting of export crops, such as artichokes, tomatoes, cotton, rice, potatoes, and other vegetables.

In the south, geological information indicates that vast quantities of water may exist far below the Sahara. The government has dug deep wells in an attempt to find these massive reserves of water. Such supplies could be tapped for several years in areas of now unproductive desert. The water, however, would not last forever, because no new water is entering the underground reservoirs.

Independent Picture Service

Locusts cling to a small tree whose leaves they have devoured. With billions of locusts moving across North Africa in 1988—the worst plague since 1954—Tunisia faced the threat of all its crops being destroyed. The cost of fighting the insects and the potential loss of farmland and farm jobs placed a serious burden on the economy.

Independent Picture Service

Irrigation, flood and erosion control, and more efficient use of the land have made the Medjerda River Valley in the north one of the most productive farming regions in Tunisia.

53

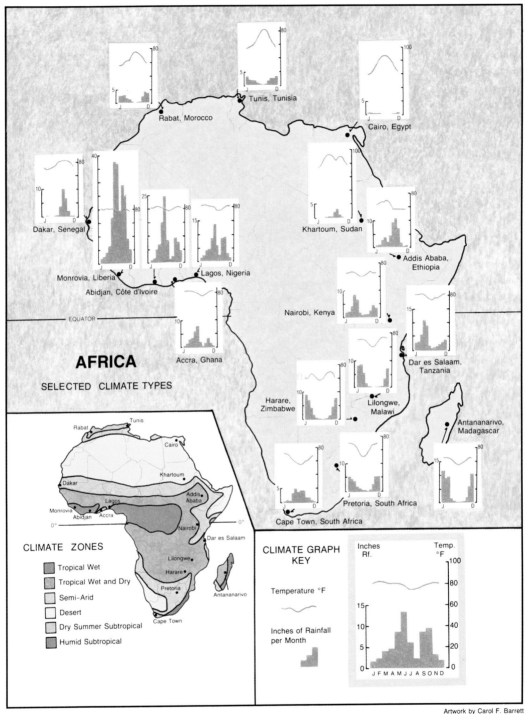

AFRICA

SELECTED CLIMATE TYPES

CLIMATE ZONES

- Tropical Wet
- Tropical Wet and Dry
- Semi-Arid
- Desert
- Dry Summer Subtropical
- Humid Subtropical

CLIMATE GRAPH KEY

Temperature °F

Inches of Rainfall per Month

Artwork by Carol F. Barrett

These climate graphs show the monthly changes in the average rainfall received and in the average temperatures from January to December for the capital cities of 16 African nations. Tunis, Tunisia, has the hot, dry summers and cool, wet winters that are typical of areas around the Mediterranean Sea. Because it is on the extreme northern edge of Africa, Tunis is just beyond the edge of the Sahara Desert, making the capital wetter than Cairo, which is in the desert. Data taken from *World-Climates* by Willy Rudloff, Stuttgart, 1981.

Agricultural workers gather grapes in northern Tunisia. Until 1964 when Tunisia nationalized French landholdings, almost all of the nation's grapes were processed into wine and exported to France. Although the loss of the French market has greatly reduced wine production, grapes are still cultivated on a small scale.

Manufacturing and Fishing

The Tunisian government has encouraged the development of export-oriented industries. Chemical plants, mainly in the south near the sources of phosphates, produce fertilizers and other products largely for foreign markets. Local petroleum plants in Bizerte and Gabès refine about half of the oil for domestic needs and export the rest to overseas markets.

Along Tunisia's coasts, fishermen catch hauls of fish, which are sold in markets throughout the country or are frozen for export.

55

Food processing—including vegetable and fish canning and the production of sugar, flour, and wines—also earns Tunisia foreign money. Local markets sell processed foods along with fresh agricultural products. The development of manufacturing firms, such as a steel plant and a paper mill, provides new jobs to reduce unemployment.

Many small-scale consumer industries operate throughout the country. Local, cooperatively owned companies, for example, may employ 20 to 50 people, who produce foods, soft drinks, plastic goods, soap, clothing, or furniture. French investors founded many of these enterprises, which came under local control after the nationalization of foreign-owned businesses in the 1960s.

The Mediterranean offers Tunisia a wide variety of fish and shellfish, which factories process both for domestic consumption and for export. Almost every village along the coast specializes in some kind of fishing. Sponges, which are exported to France and to Eastern European countries, are important along the southern coast from Sfax to Gabès and on the islands of Kerkenna and Jerba. Fishermen catch sardines along the Gulf of Hammamet and tuna along the Gulf of Tunis, especially at the village of Sidi Daoud.

Great strength is required to pull in the huge nets full of fish caught off Tunisian shores.

Courtesy of Embassy of Tunisia

56

At Shatt al-Jerid, workers load a truck with salt, which has been obtained by open-air evaporation of sea water. The mineral meets both domestic needs and export demands.

Mining

Tunisia is one of the world's largest suppliers of phosphate. Most of the country's phosphate reserves are located in remote areas around the oasis town of Gafsa, which makes the mineral expensive to mine. Government-owned factories that produce fertilizers and other phosphate chemicals (which are more marketable than the raw mineral) have led to increased phosphate mining. In the mid-1980s output of the unprocessed mineral was about five million tons a year. The phosphate industry experienced worldwide overproduction in the 1980s, and both exports and prices have dropped since then.

Although petroleum production has never reached levels comparable to those of neighboring Algeria and Libya, Tunisia produces more than five million tons of crude oil annually. A decline in oil prices during the 1980s hurt the Tunisian economy. Natural gas fields near Cape Bon meet the energy needs of Tunis. Minerals such as lead, zinc, and salt are also mined.

Home Industries

The Tunisian government has helped to organize traditional home industries into cooperatives, which have increased output and have found foreign markets for finished products. Carpets and blankets, especially those from Kairouan and Gafsa, have been highly valued since merchants first took them to trade in faraway cities, such as Cairo, Egypt, and Fès, Morocco.

Craftspeople still handweave these products on antique looms in traditional patterns of bright blues and reds. Tourists buy many of the carpets and blankets, and others are exported to Europe where they command high prices. Additional home industries include those that produce leather goods, pottery, basketry, and brass and olive-wood utensils.

57

Carpet knotters in Kairouan produce intricately patterned rugs that borrow from Persian design.

Rugs are also woven in Kairouan, the hub of Tunisia's carpet industry.

A potter carefully turns a vase at his shop on Jerba Island, where a community of artists thrives.

A display of finished pottery features brightly painted wares that have been fired in a hot oven.

With nimble fingers a craftsperson from Monastir deftly weaves a basket from local grasses.

59

Transportation

The Romans were the first to develop an inland transportation system in Tunisia. Several centuries later, the French also made efforts to improve the country's land routes. Paved national highways now cover over 13,000 miles. Roads are generally kept in passable condition, but in the south, where windstorms sometimes cover roads with sand, weeks may go by before the routes are cleared for traffic. Besides a bus system, independently owned station-wagon taxis called *louages* (French for "rentals") connect most towns.

A flood in 1970 washed away much of the 1,500-mile railway system in the south, and Tunisia's train network is still being repaired. Railroads still connect most of the leading cities and tourist attractions along the eastern coast. About 85 percent of the rail service transports freight, and the rest carries passengers.

Several international airlines, including Tunisia's own Tunis Air, link the city of Tunis with major European airports and have occasional flights to New York. Domestic airlines fly from Tunis to Sfax, Jerba, and Tozeur. The Tunis-Carthage Airport opened in 1972 and can serve two million passengers a year. French and Italian steamships connect Tunis with Nice in France, with Naples in Italy, and with the island of Sicily.

Foreign Trade

Despite efforts during the 1970s and 1980s to make Tunisia self-sufficient, the country still buys more goods from foreign countries than the nation sells to them. Traditionally, Tunisian industry and business depended on France for both imports and exports. Disputes between the two nations—especially when Tunisia national-

Independent Picture Service

South of the Sahel, Tunisia's main highway runs into the flat, arid expanses of the south. When the wind blows, the pavement is sometimes lost beneath layers of fine, yellow sand.

Tunisia's rural inhabitants often travel by foot, using donkeys or camels to transport goods.

ized land owned by French citizens—have caused France to end the tax benefits it once gave to Tunisia. France still buys Tunisian goods and supplies some of its imports, but the French no longer dominate Tunisian trade.

West Germany, Italy, France, and the United States buy substantial quantities of Tunisian exports, and these same countries also supply many of Tunisia's imported goods. Besides raw phosphate and phosphate products, Tunisia exports olives,

Fishermen dock their boats at Cape Bon, the port from which some of their catch will be exported to foreign countries.

The many ports along Tunisia's coasts have been vital to the nation's economy since the days of the Phoenicians.

In addition to balmy Mediterranean beaches, a long history and extensive ruins attract visitors to Tunisia. This mosque in Tunis exhibits some of the variety of influences on Tunisia's architectural styles.

olive oil, wine, petroleum, and textiles. Food and machinery account for much of the nation's foreign purchases.

Tourism

Promoting the excellent beaches along its eastern coast as well as the wealth of its Roman, Byzantine, and Arab ruins, Tunisia has successfully lured visitors from across the Mediterranean. The government has built resort hotels and has encouraged private investors from Germany and France to build still others. As a result, the number of foreign visitors has risen to more than one million per year.

People from France, Italy, and Scandinavia make up the largest percentage of visitors to Tunisia. Tourists from Eastern Europe, especially from Yugoslavia, enjoy traveling to the country because their money can buy more in Tunisia than in their own countries. Many coastal resorts, such as Hammamet, Monastir, and Houmt Souk, offer a comfortable climate throughout the year.

The tourist industry declined in the mid-1980s after the Israeli raid on the PLO headquarters in Tunis and after the rise of Libyan-sponsored terrorism. Nevertheless, tourism remains a major source of foreign currency.

The Future

Amid already high unemployment and inflation rates, Tunisia faced further economic difficulties in the 1980s. A drought and a locust plague have affected agriculture, and earnings from tourism, phosphate, and oil have declined. Although the country has undergone rapid social and technological development since 1956, conservative Tunisians are questioning the value of these changes when economic gains have not matched the improvements.

Former president Bourguiba succeeded in keeping Tunisia stable under his guidance, but many Tunisians believe that the government must become more open if progress is to continue. The nation's large number of unemployed and underemployed university graduates could become Tunisia's greatest asset if the government can find a way to use them as a resource. It remains to be seen whether Bourguiba's successor—Zine al-Abidine ben Ali—can meet these economic, social, and political challenges. With strong, sensible leadership Tunisia could take a prominent place in the Arab world as well as a leadership role in North Africa.

Tunisians are generally optimistic about their country since Zine al-Abidine ben Ali took over the government in late 1987. Unlike former president Bourguiba, ben Ali, who is a devout Muslim, focuses on improving relations with Arab states. Tunisians hope the new approach will enable the nation to serve as an economic, geographic, and political link between Africa, the Middle East, and Europe.

Courtesy of Embassy of Tunisia

Index